HISTORY

Since the mists of time, the rock has always been sacred. As a place of Celtic worship, frontiers between the earth and the hereafter should be abolished on the day of Samain.

It was originally called Mount Tombe, from the latin tumba and from the celtic tum which means « high place ».

In the 6th century, Christian hermits built two sanctuaries dedicated respectively to Saint-Symphorien and to Saint-Etienne. A Saint-Symphorien spring actually rises up outside, at the base of the ramparts between north tower and Boucle tower.

When they were gnawed by hunger, the hermits lit a fire out of green branches. A thick smoke then rose up and thus warned the priest of Asteriac (now Beauvoir). He loaded a donkey with food which carved its way on its own down to Mount Tombe. But a wolf came one day and devoured the donkey.

Heavenly wrath exploded and the Powers above compelled the wolf to take the place of the donkey in the hermits' service.

One night in 708, the bishop of Avranches, Aubert, had an amazing dream : the Archangel Saint-Michael, Prince of the heavenly hosts, appeared to him and ordered him to erect and consecrate a sanctuary to him. Convinced that he had had a vision of the Devil, the priest did nothing but prayed fervently.

The Archangel appeared again, with no more success. At his third appea-rance, Saint-Michael put his holy finger on Aubert's head « so that he poked a hole in it through which one could see the brains » (Dom Thomas Le Roy, a Benedictine monk of the 17th century).

The relic and its shrine.

Saint-Aubert's skull is a piece of the treasure of the Saint-Gervais Basilica in Avranches.

Photos : Municipal Library of Avranches

The Archangel told the now convinced bishop that he would have to edify this sanctuary at the very place where a bull which had been stolen and tied up would be discovered. The oratory should be as large as the area which had been trampled by the bull and been kept dry, despite the dew.

But a huge stone, probably a dolmen, was standing on this very spot and nothing could move it. It was the child Bain, the twelfth son of a worker, who managed with his foot to knock it down. According to legend, the Saint-Aubert chapel of the 15th century which is situated at west at the foot of the rock was erected on this stone that only a miracle could have allowed to rush down the slope.

Then the sanctuary could be built. Based on a round plan, it is shaped like a cave and can accomodate a hundred people. It is the counterpart of the cave on Monte Gargano, in the south of Italy. There Saint-Michael appeared for the first time in the west, at the end of the 5th century.

By order of Aubert, a college of twelve canons settled on the Mount and worshipped Saint-Michael. Two emissaries were sent to Monte Gargano to bring back Saint-Michael's relics. They came back a year later with a piece of cloth and a fragment of a stone upon which he had stood. The sanctuary was consecrated on 6th October 709. From it remains a cyclopean wall visible behind one of the altars in Our-Lady-Underground, the Preromanesque church of the 10th century.

The Saint-Aubert's chapel, built in the 15th century.

Photo : Daniel Quérel

MONT-SAINT-MICHEL, LAND OF LEGENDS, OR THE BIRTH OF A CULT

THE MOUNT BECOMES NORMAN

At a time when France did not exist, still less Normandy, the Mount was incorporated into Austrasia. The realms of Neustria on the west and Austrasia on the east were reunified by Pepin. In the face of more and more numerous inroads by the Vikings, Charles-le-Simple gave to the Breton Salomon the charge of Cotentin, of which the Mount is a dependency. The treaty of Saint-Clair-sur-Epte between Charles-le-Simple and Rollon, chief of Normans, founded Normandy in 911. The Cotentin was not annexed before 933.

In 966, Richard I, Duke of Normandy, accused the canons of numerous sins and threw them out. Their only fault was to have maintained good relations with their Breton neighbours. Twelve Benedictine monks from Saint-Wandrille then settled in the Mount with Mainard as their abbot. Over the centuries, the abbey has been richly endowed by the dukes of Normandy not to mention by lords worried about the salvation of their souls, by the gifts of the faithfull, finally by the kings of France.

It became a seigneury ruling over a wide estate.

The Couesnon river which, according to a saying, «foolishly put the Mount in Normandy».

Photo : Pierre-Marie Aubertel

HISTORY

The English troops of King Edward III Plantagenet landed in Saint-Vaast-la-Hougue in 1346. They looted and spread terror in their wake : the Hundred Years' War began.

The English captured Tombelaine rock for the first time in 1357. The future Charles VI gave the abbots of the Mount the title of captain. One of them, Robert Jolivet, set about erecting fortifications in 1417. The disloyal abbot changed sides after having been bribed.

The English came back in the region of Manche in 1418. In September 1425, Louis d'Estouteville, a loyal and faithfull knight, became the captain of Mont-Saint-Michel. Accompanied by 119 other knights, he was the glorious defender of the place and undertook important work in order to strengthen the defences of the site. His body lies in the abbey of Hambye.

Abbey of Hambye.

Photo : P. Lelièvre - CDT de la Manche

View of the bay and Tombelaine with the pinnacles of the choir in the foreground.

All the West of France was occupied by the English except Mont-Saint-Michel. It soon became the symbol of resistance to the English. The King of England desperately wanted to capture the Archangel's Sanctuary. The enemy was on Tombelaine rock and fortified it, and settled fortresses in Genets, Saint-Leonard and Ardevon. The siege lasted over 19 years but the besieged, under the authority and leadership of Louis of Estouteville, beat off all the assaults and even launched attacks when necessary.

On June 17th 1434, a fire broke out in the village and the Englishman Thomas of Scale immediately gathered an army. An attack was launched, a breach being made when Estouteville and his knights suddenly appeared and compelled the English to retreat. This was victory, with two English bombards called « Michelets » as a war trophy. These lie still on their carriage at the entrance of the Mount.

The heroic resistance of the inhabitants of the Mount reinvigorated supporters of the King of France. A year later, Granville was set free.

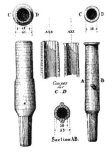

Photo : Daniel Quérel

The two English bombards (15th century).

Remains of building on Tombelaine.

The setting up of commendam in 1516 and thereafter led to the decline of the abbey. The abbot was no longer elected by the monks but directly appointed by the king ; he received his revenue from the abbey without having to live on the Mount. Some of these commendatory abbots were laymen who preferred to live at court.

Monks were left to themselves and morals loosened. They neglected services, wore lace collars and cuffs, went for hunting and frequented taverns. Pilgrims became fewer.

Later, monks from Saint-Maur came and settled in the Mount in 1622 and restored calm. The abbey achieved spiritual and intellectual renewal afterwards.

The abbey and the ramparts were registered as « historic monuments » in 1874. Important restoration works were undertaken in order to restore the site. The first architects in chief were Edouard Corroyer, Victor Petitgrand who built the bell tower and the spire, and Paul Gout. Pilgrimages started again in 1865 along with those of the diocese of Coutances ; and friars from Saint-Edme-de-Pontigny

took up there their residence from 1867 to 1886.

In 1969, shortly after the monastic Millenium, a small Benedictine community settled down. Thanks to their presence, their payers, to the services and mass that they celebrate everyday, the abbey has recovered its spiritual grandeur.

Photo : Père Fr. Lancelot

The main street with its shops and their signboards.

A PRISON

Louis XI converted a part of the abbey into a prison equiped with an iron cage. In the 17th century, it was called « the Bastille of the sea ». Pamphleteers, Jansenists and people imprisoned on order under the King's private seal were confined into the small or the big « Exile », as the cells used to be called.

After Revolution, in 1793, three hundred priests who declined to take an oath before the civil constitution were sent to prison in the Mount. This one was then renamed the « Free Mount ».

In 1811, the abbey was turned into a county gaol then in 1817 into a prison and a reformatory for men and women sentenced to hard labour or deportation. Then the buildings were arranged into weaving workrooms or hat and shoe factories : the abbey was mutilated. Victor Hugo said about the prison that it was « a toad in the middle of a reliquary ».

The prison for women was established in the hostellery of Robert of Thorigny but collapsed in 1818. Huge butresses strengthened its ruins in 1863.

From 1793 to 1863, fourteen thousand prisoners stayed in the Mount ; some of them died there.

The most famous prisoners were Le Carpentier, Blanqui, Barbes. The prison was eventually closed by Napoleon III in 1874 despite the petitions that the inhabitants sent out, fearing that they might lose a valuable source of income.

The beginning of tourism gave a new boost to the village economy. In their own way people of Mont-Saint-Michel perpetuate a millenial tradition in trade and the hotel business.

The illustration shows Louis-Auguste Blanqui in his cell. Municipal Library of Avranches

One of the first places of Christendom after Jerusalem, Rome and Saint-Jacques-de-Compostelle, Mont-Saint-Michel welcomed more and more pilgrims yet without succeeding in rivalizing with Saint-Jacques-de-Compostelle.

If a proverb says that « little beggars go to Mont-Saint-Michel while the big ones go to Saint-Jacques », the kings of France, up to Charles IX, came and payed homage to the sanctuary of the Archangel. Some of them, like Saint-Louis, Louis XI and François I, came several times.

Pilgrims, also called « miquelots », arrived from all over Europe on the pathways of the Mount (also called the ways of paradise) which were marked out with monasteries, welcoming shelters. They wore a cape, carried a leather sack on their shoulders and leant on a staff. Nearby the Mount, a sanitary cordon encircled the bay with leper-hospitals and lazar-houses.

Finally the wave of pilgrims broke over the strand before the final ascent towards the light and sanctuary of the Archangel.

Photo : SMET - CDT 50 - André Mauxion

Crossing the bay with the guides of «Maison de la Baie».

PILGRIMAGES

Whatever the motivation of these men, women - and even sometimes children - either a spiritual quest, a deep devotion, or thanks to offer, or a penance or a serious offence to expiate, all of them had to face a hazardous crossing fraught with dangers : the fog which isolated and misled, the quicksands which swallowed up, the flood-tide which drowned the unwary.

« Mont-Saint-Michel in Peril of the sea » was a justified name, alas. In 1318, in a single day, thirteen pilgrims were suffocated to death in the crowd, eighteen drowned and another twelve disappeared in quicksands!

During the Hundred Years' War, the English who had occupied Tombelaine rock had forbidden all pilgrimages, then only to the Normans as potential accomplices, finally granting free access to everyone but the Normans, provided that visitors pay a fee.

SOUVENIRS

First pilgrims took fragments of stone away from the edifice, a habit that fortunately enough the canons quickly forbade.

Then they collected sand or shells before there began a whole trade of phials filled with sand, necklaces made of shells, and of medals or signs also called « leads » : these were shells of tin or lead bearing the effigy of Saint-Michael overwhelming the dragon. They were sewn on to hats or garments.

These shells are on the coat of arms of the abbey, crowned by lilies (on the right when entering the abbey church).

Mould for pilgrimage signs with the effigy of Saint-Michael (15th century). Engraved schist. J. Laurette, a craftsman in Ardevon, discovered it by chance (8 cm high, 4 cm large and 2 cm thick).

Photo : Daniel Quérel

OUR-LADY-UNDERGROUND

Built during the 10th century on the slopes of the rock, Our-Lady-Underground was to be merged into the foundations of the abbey church of which it was to support the nave in the 11th century.

It was disfigured in the 18th century by a partition wall meant to bed the frontage of the new church.
Architect Paul Gout rediscovered it in 1908 during some excavations and it was extricated only in 1960, by Yves-Marie Froidevaux. The supporting wall was pulled down, afterwards the five hundred tons of façade are supported by two concrete girders.

Our-Lady-Underground has two naves whose choirs are topped with the galleries where the relics probably used to be exhibited. The two altars were respectively dedicated to the Blessed Virgin and to the Holy Trinity.

Alternate layers of flat bricks and of stones are peculiar to Carolingian architecture.
Behind the altars appears a cyclopean wall which is a vestige of the sanctuary of abbot Aubert.

The Preromanesque church Our-Lady-Underground.

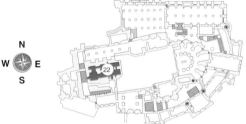

Intermediate floor

N
W E
S

22

THE ROMANESQUE ABBEY

The Romanesque abbey's role was not only to welcome more and more pilgrims while enforcing the monastic enclosure but also to show and assert the powers of Norman dukes in this border place.

So, the conventual buildings stand in tiers on sides of the rock while the abbey church dominates the top of it.

The plan of the abbey church realised by Jaussaud in 1957.

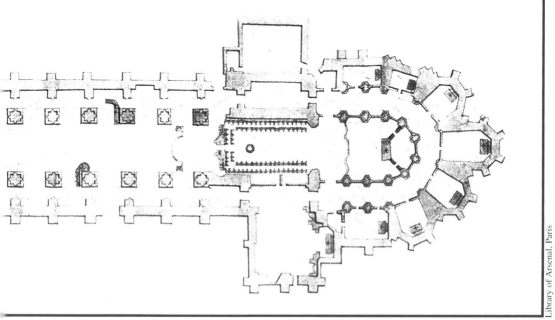

ARCHITECTURE

THE ABBEY CHURCH

The abbey church was built on the top of the originally cone-shaped rock. Since this is 80 metres high, the church was to be 80 metres long. The abbey church is thus set into a square which is the symbol of the Created world.

The first difficulty to get over in carrying out this project was to cope with the narrowness of the top by creating a huge artifical platform. The church has the shape of the latin cross. The middle part, the crossing of transept, lies on the very top of the rock which has been slightly levelled. Crypts were built on east, south and north slopes so that they supported the choir and both of the arms of the transept. The fourth crypt existed already : it is the Preromanesque church. It has been strengthened and now supports the nave which was originally longer. Work began in 1023 and lasted up to 1080, which makes about 60 years.

The Mount in 1701. This model is exhibited in the Museum of relief maps in Hotel des Invalides in Paris.

The Romanesque nave and the Flamboyant Gothic choir.

Top floor

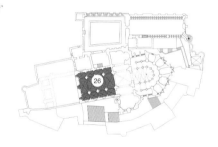

THE NAVE

The nave is typical of Norman naves with its three levels : tall arcades, galleries, and high windows above. It is topped with a beam roof : the use of wood, lighter than stone, allowed the building of tall and very opened walls. Side aisles were covered with groined vaults. The north wall collapsed in 1103. It was rebuilt at the beginning of the 12th century. The relieving archs surmounting the high windows of the south wall have been left derelict, and the packing of the first level of the arches with stuffed mortar was replaced by bonded stone.

The nave no longer includes seven bays as originally but four which are marked off by the engaged half-columns. In 1776, fire damaged the first three bays which were near to collapse. Maurists, monks in the Mount at that time, decided to pull them down and have the present neoclassical façade with its Romanesque capitals built in 1780. The three former bays are now marked by some small rises in the ground.

The Romanesque nave was preceded by a narthex. It had been modified in the 12th century and set off with two towers under the abbacy of Robert of Thorigny who happened to be a famous abbot but not such a good builder for both of these ended by collapsing.

ARCHITECTURE

THE TRANSEPT

The whole crossing was rebuilt in the 19th century. The north arm of the transept had been shortened in the 13th century during the erection of cloisters. But the south arm of the transept remained untouched.

Statue of the 11th century of Saint-Michael, in the transept. In Hebrew, Mi-ka-el means « who is like God ». This is what Saint-Michael shouted when Lucifer, the fallen angel, pretended being equal to God. A fight ensued and Lucifer fell in abyss. The archangel is represented holding a balance for he weighs and guides souls on doomsday.

THE FLAMBOYANT GOTHIC CHOIR

In 1421, in the middle of the Hundred Years' War, while the English were based on Tombelaine islet, the Romanesque chancel collapsed. Raised up to five metres higher than the church entrance, it included an ambulatory.

The construction of the present choir began 25 years later and was not completed before 1521, that is to say a whole century after its collapse.

On the outside, very graceful flying butresses support the chancel.

Fine colonnettes upon the piles of the chancel spring 25 metres up to the high windows without anything to interrupt their ascent. The eye is seized by light. For if God is Light, the Archangel is the chief of the Light forces.

Top floor

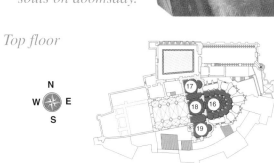

N
W E
S

16. Choir
17. North arm of the transept
18. Crossing
19. South arm of the transept

LOCATION VIEW

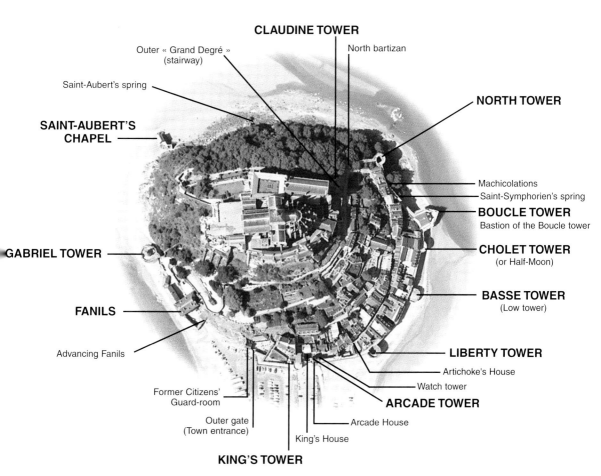

CLAUDINE TOWER

North bartizan

Outer « Grand Degré »
(stairway)

Saint-Aubert's spring

NORTH TOWER

**SAINT-AUBERT'S
CHAPEL**

Machicolations
Saint-Symphorien's spring

BOUCLE TOWER
Bastion of the Boucle tower

GABRIEL TOWER

CHOLET TOWER
(or Half-Moon)

BASSE TOWER
(Low tower)

FANILS

Advancing Fanils

LIBERTY TOWER

Artichoke's House

Watch tower

ARCADE TOWER

Former Citizens'
Guard-room

Outer gate
(Town entrance)

Arcade House

King's House

KING'S TOWER

Photos : Philippe Pique

15

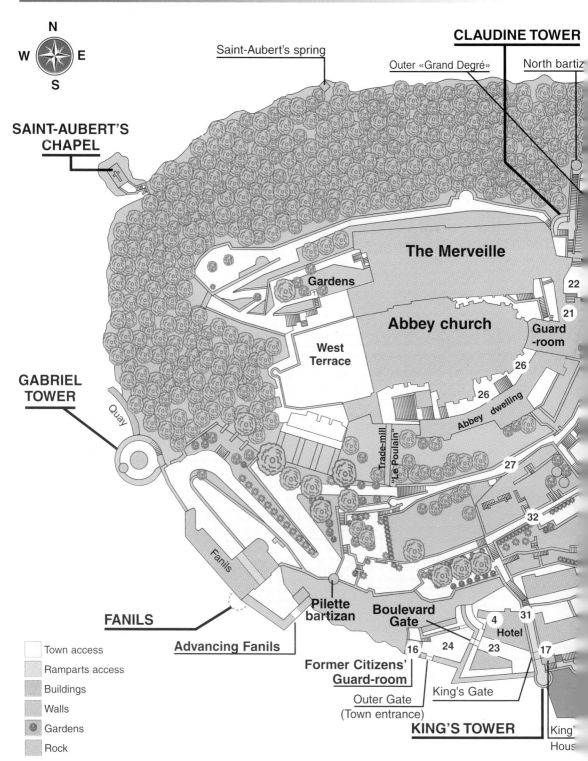

N
W   E
S

SAINT-AUBERT'S CHAPEL

Saint-Aubert's spring

CLAUDINE TOWER

Outer «Grand Degré»

North bartiz

GABRIEL TOWER

Quay

The Merveille

Gardens

Abbey church

West Terrace

22
21
Guard -room
26
26
Abbey dwelling
27
32

Trade-mill "Le Poulain"

Fanils

FANILS

Pilette bartizan

Boulevard Gate

4
Hotel
31

Advancing Fanils

16
24
23
17

Former Citizens' Guard-room

King's Gate

Outer Gate (Town entrance)

KING'S TOWER

King Hous

☐ Town access
☐ Ramparts access
☐ Buildings
☐ Walls
☐ Gardens
☐ Rock

SAINT-MICHEL

NORTH TOWER

Machicolations

Saint-Symphorien's spring

BOUCLE TOWER

Bastion of the Boucle tower

CHOLET TOWER

(or Half-Moon)

BASSE TOWER

(Low tower)

LIBERTY TOWER

Artichoke's House

Watch Tower

Arcade House

ARCADE TOWER

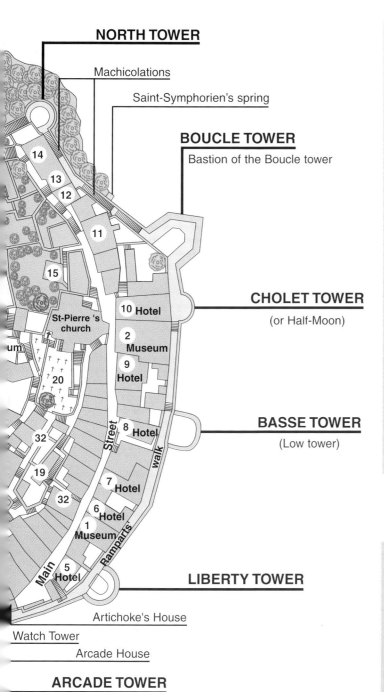

14
13
12
11
15
10 Hotel
St-Pierre's church
2 Museum
9 Hotel
um
20
32
8 Hotel
19
7 Hotel
32
6 Hotel
1 Museum
Street
walk
Ramparts
Main
5 Hotel

Key

1 . . . . . Historical and Maritime
. . . . Museum
2 . . . . Archeoscope
3 . . . . Grévin Museum
4 . . . . La Mère Poulard
5 . . . . Le Saint-Pierre
6 . . . . La Croix Blanche
7 . . . . Le Duguesclin
8 . . . . Le Mouton Blanc
9 . . . . La Vieille Auberge
10 . . . . . Les Terrasses Poulard
11 . . . . Le Vieux Logis
12 . . . . Logis Saint-Symphorien
13 . . . . Logis Saint-Aubert
14 . . . . . Logis du Pigeon Blanc
15 . . . . Logis Tiphaine (museum)
16 . . . . Tourist Office
17 . . . . Town Hall
18 . . . . Post Office
19 . . . . Lectures Hall
20 . . . . Graveyard
21 . . . . Chatelet (the Fort)
22 . . . . Barbican
23 . . . . . Barbican or Boulevard
24 . . . . Outpost Courtyard
25 . . . . Former « Hôtellerie de la
. . . . Licorne »
26 . . . . . Indoor « Grand Degré »
27 . . . . Abbey watchpath
28 . . . . Barbican watchpath
29 . . . . Jerusalem's Cross
30 . . . . Former « Hôtellerie de la
. . . . Truie qui File»
. . . . . . (literally the Spinning Sow)
31 . . . . Monteux stairs
32 . . . . Alleys

Figures of the Mount

Perimeter of the Mount : 1 km
Altitude of the Abbey (from sea average level) : 80 m
Height of the Archange statue from its plinth to its sword : 4.5 m
The only Archangel : 2.8 m
Weight : 450 kg
Distance between the Mount and Tombelaine : 2.8 km

PLANS OF THE ABBEY

• **Top floor**

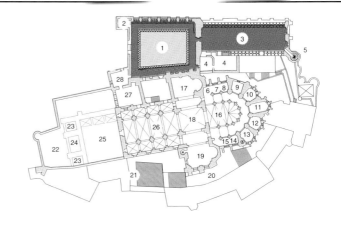

• **Intermediate floor**

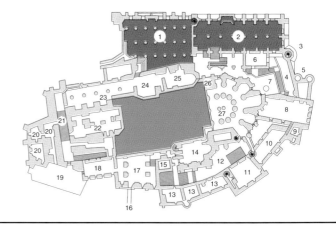

• **Lower floor**

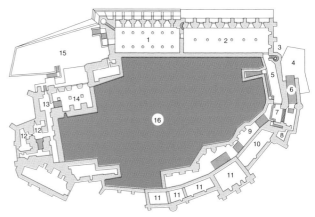

KEY

1 Cloister
2 Archives
3 Refectory
4 Kitchens
5 Corbins' tower
6 Sacristie
7 Saint-André's chapel
8 Saint-Scubilion's chapel
9 Saint-Michel-le-Petit chapel

10 Saint-Pierre's chapel
11 Our-Lady chapel
12 Sainte-Anne's chapel
13 Saint-Martin's chapel
14 Saint-Pair's chapel
15 Saint-Aubert's chapel
16 Choir
17 North arm of the transept
18 Crossing
19 South arm of the transept

20 Indoor Grand Degré
21 Gauthier Leap
22 Plomb du Four
23 Towers (missing)
24 Portal (missing)
25 Bays (missing)
26 Nave
27 Dormitory
28 Infirmary

---

1 Knights' hall
  (or scriptorium)
2 Guests' hall
3 Corbins' tower
4 The Merveille courtyard
5 Chatelet (the Fort)
6 Saint-Madeleine's chapel
7 Cistern and garden
8 Belle-Chaise court-room
9 Perrine tower

10 Abbey dwelling
11 Abbey dwelling
12 Indoor Grand Degré
13 Abbey dwelling
14 Saint-Martin's crypt
15 Cistern
16 The poulain (trade-mill)
17 Former ossuary
18 Saint-Etienne's chapel
19 Hostellery (missing)

20 Lodgings of Robert
   of Thorigny
21 North-South passageway
22 Our-Lady-Underground
23 The Promenoir
24 Devil's dungeon
25 The Thirty Candles crypt
26 Cistern
27 Great Pillars crypt

---

1 Cellar
2 Almonry
3 The Corbins' tower
4 Barbican
5 The Merveille courtyard
6 Chatelet and the Pit steps

7 Guard-room
8 Perrine tower
9 Indoor Grand Degré
10 Lodging of the baillif
11 Abbey dwelling
12 Dungeons

13 Romanesque entrance
14 Aquilon's room
(Romanesque almonry)
15 North gardens
16 Natural rock

ARCHITECTURE

THE GREAT PILLARS CRYPT

Huge pillars, nearly six metres round, stand up as a forest of stones.

Ambulatory and radiating chapels reproduce here the plan of the Flamboyant Gothic choir. The crypt leads to the magnificent court-room of Belle-Chaise.

The Great Pillars crypt.

Photo : Père Fr. Lancelot

Intermediate floor

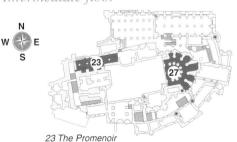

N
W E
S

23

27

23 The Promenoir
27 The Great Pillars crypt

THE PROMENOIR

The main remaining conventual building rises at the north of the nave up to three floors and includes the Aquilon room, the Promenoir and the dormitory.

So-called in the 19th century, this room in all likelyhood answered to the purposes of refectory, chapter-house or scriptorium. A row of median columns with monolithic shafts parts it into two naves. All that remains in the thickness of the wall is the entrance for a passage, an indoor watchpath. The intersective rib vaults, built after the north wall of the nave had collapsed, are among the very first ones built in Normandy.

The Promenoir.

THE WHEEL

Evidence of the time when it was a prison, the treadmill installed in the ossuary in the 19th century allowed the prison to be supplied with food and materials. Prisoners used to set it into motion by walking inside it. A trolley connected to the wheel by a cable slid down the ramp and out.

This method, known by Romans, has been used on all sites of the Middle Ages. In Mont-Saint-Michel, stones were carved at the bottom of the rock then hoisted up to the top using wheels of this sort.

Photo : Père Fr. Lancelot

The wheel (or « poulain »).

SAINT-MARTIN'S CRYPT

The atmosphere emanating from this crypt evokes that which pervades the Preromanesque church Our-Lady-Underground.

The Saint-Martin's chapel supports the south arm of the church transept. It has a half-round apse with an oven vault. The cradle-vault strengthened by a transverse arch has an exceptionnal nine metre span. Here the square meets the circle and the Created world comes near to Heaven.

Photo : Père Fr. Lancelot

Saint Martin's crypt.

Intermediate floor

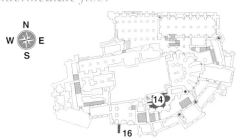

14 Saint-Martin's crypt
16 The wheel

ARCHITECTURE

In 1204, King Philippe-Auguste of France conquered Normandy, which until then made one whole state with England. But the monastic community kept its faith with the King of England.

The King of France's ally, the Breton Guy de Thouars, decided out of zeal to besiege Mont-Saint-Michel. His troops could not manage to take hold of the Mount and set fire to the village before leaving. Fire quickly spread over up to the top : the abbey was damaged. To have this sacrilege forgiven, Philippe-Auguste generously endowed the abbey, which was to help to build the Marvel.

The Gothic monastery was erected under the abbacies of Jourdain, Ranulphe de l'Isle, Thomas des Chambres and Raoul de Villedieu.

Only seventeen years were enough to raise on the north side both of the three-storeyed buildings which represent the medieval hierarchy. The east building includes the almonry, the guests' hall, the refectory : those who work, those who fight, those who pray. And the west building comprises the cellar, the Knights' hall (scriptorium), the cloisters : materialistic, intellectual and spiritual life.

The Flamboyant Gothic choir.

Photo : Père Fr. Lancelot

The Merveille, north façade.

The Merveille.

THE GOTHIC ABBEY

THE ALMONRY

Divided in two naves and roofed with groined vaults, the almonry is characterized by its plainness : capitals are bare, without any ornament. Humbler people were received in this room probably dating from the 12th century.

THE CELLAR

Supplies were preserved in this cool dark room. The groined vaulting comes down above square pillars. The original plaster cast realized by Fremiet for the famous statue of the Archangel stands majestically in the room.

It enabled the staff of the Monduit work-shop to make the statue which has been topping the spire since 6th August 1897. This chased-copper statue was restored in 1987 and covered with a gold-leaf. The points of the wings and of the sword act as lightning-rods, which happens to be very useful in a place where lightning has started many fires over the centuries. It is 4.50 metres tall and weighs 450 kilograms. It was lowered by a helicopter and carried up again in the same way.

The plaster cast realized by Fremiet stands in the cellar.

Lower floor

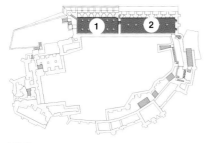

1 Cellar
2 Almonry

ARCHITECTURE

THE KNIGHTS' HALL

The Scriptorium, or the Knights' hall, is divided into three naves by stout columns. Sunken mouldings are very pronounced, the ornament of the round abacus capitals evokes plants and the profile of arches is underlined with very deep grooves. The scriptorium was assigned to the copying out and illuminating of manuscripts.

At the time of the Revolution, the town of Avranches received the books of the abbey on trust. Among these, there were two hundred manuscripts. This is one of the most important collections for the Romanesque period in Europe. Some of them are exhibited in the Ancient Fund library in the town-hall of Avranches.

A heightened gallery is arranged in the south. It was formerly closed by a partition wall so that the guests could get back to church while respecting the monastic enclosure.

Although it had been founded in the castle at Amboise by Louis XI, the Order of Saint-Michael Knights gave its name to this hall for it long has been said that their first meeting was held at Mont-Saint-Michel.

Intermediate floor

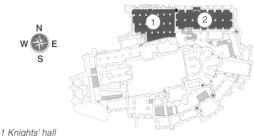

N
W E
S

1 Knights' hall
2 Guests' hall

Saint Augustin inspired by God, in the Mount's scriptorium (mid-11th century).

Photo : Municipal Library of Avranches

THE GOTHIC ABBEY

THE GUESTS' HALL

The state-room for distinguished guests is divided into naves by a row of very slim columns. It was richly ornamented with tapestries, paintings and stained-glass windows. The floor was paved with enamelled tiling emblazoned with the arms of France and Castille : princely ostentation and architectural elegance were reserved for prominent guests. These could meditate in the Saint-Madeleine's chapel before their having meal.

Both of the monumental fireplaces were used as kitchens. Their lintels are bonded with Jove joints.

Photo : Père Fr. Lancelot

he Knights' hall.

Initial letter Q for Quoniam, in Saint-Jérôme and Saint-Ambroise writings (11th, folio 122).

Municipal Library of Avranches

Photo : Père Fr. Lancelot

The Guests' hall.

ARCHITECTURE

THE CLOISTERS

Building work ended with the construction of the cloisters in 1228.

At the top floor of the west building, cloisters are suspended between sky and ground, like a closed space lending itself to meditation, and yet opening on to the sky. Their lightness is enhanced by the fineness of the colonnettes. Set out in a quincunx, their double row makes tripods and ensures an even and light distribution of loads upon the vaults of the lower floor.

Originally made out of lumachel (fire-marble) imported from England, they were replaced in the 19th century by pudding-stone from La Lucerne (in Manche).

The frieze, arranged as a tapestry, consists in a multitude of flowers and plants motifs and turns in the north gallery into a real stone-lace.
Sculptors Maître Jean and Maître Roger left us their faces carved in the Caen-stone in the west gallery. The openings, glazed by now, bear witness to a project for a third building on the west side which finally dropped.

Cloisters, an enclosed place appropriate for contemplation.

Top floor

1 Cloisters
3 Refectory

Photo : Père Fr. Lancelot

THE REFECTORY

The eye is at once amazed by space and luminousness of this room like a huge vessel made up of only one nave.

Side walls look plain. Actually they are pierced out of a series of narrow windows which appear only when one walks down the room. Thus pierced with windows, walls still remain strong enough to hold the weight of the super-structure.

Monks used to eat their meals in silence and not only fed their bodies but also their souls. « Recto tono » readings of holy texts were made from the lectern opened into the south wall, on the right.

In this room where light prevails, the least sound is amplified, spurts out and rebounds.

The south-west corner leads to the kitchen which was removed by the time of the Maurists. A hoist was set into the stonework and used to bring food down to the almonry.

Photo : Père Fr. Lancelot

Photo : Père Fr. Lancelot

ARCHITECTURE

THE MOUNT, A FORTIFIED TOWN

Mont-Saint-Michel was besieged four times during its history.

In 1091 when William the Conqueror died, his succession provoked a clash between his sons. Henri Beauclerc, who took refuge in the Mount, was besieged by his two brothers Robert de Courteheuse and Guillaume Le Roux, who could not help, out of brotherly courtesy, bringing him a cask when there was no wine left.

In 1204, the Mount was besieged by the Breton ally of the King of France, Guy de Thouars, then by English troops during the Hundred Years' War, then, six times running, by the Protestant soldiers of Gabriel de Montgomery during the Wars of Religion. The Mount eventually proved impregnable.

A walk on the ramparts allows the eye to take in the bay and, according to the whims of the light and the weather, one can see the Norman coast and Tombelaine rock, this sphinx laying on the strand and surrounded by the flood tide.

Beatrix tower (or Liberty tower).

Gabriel tower.

Basse tower.

North tower.

« He glimpsed the deep gash of the main street, then the sharp bristle of gables which stopped dead, tightly girded by ramparts. »
Roger Vercel

Photo : Père Fr. Lancelot

Chatelet (the Fort).

Half-Moon or Cholet tower.

THE MOUNT, A FORTIFIED TOWN

Fortifications are visible on the east and south slopes of the rock. Being very steep, the latter makes a natural defence towards north and west. Some excavations showed that the ramparts were based upon the « tangue » (a very peculiar slimy sea-sand) and not on the rock as it used to be thought. The foundations of the ramparts stand on a bank. So strengthened, the most fragile part of the wall holds out all the better against the attacks of the battering ram, and the projectiles thrown out of the machicolations could ricochet on the enemy.

From the 16th century onwards, there were three gates to pass through before entering the village. The last one, the King's tower, is a traditionnal defensive work. It consists in a double-door carriage gate closed with a portcullis, together with a gate for pedestrians. These were preceded by a drawbridge and a moat. The towers have projecting angles which allowed angles of fire to be varied. The Arcade tower still has a shingled roof, just as the Artichoke's House which proudly spans the main street. The curtain walls are perforated with machicolations, slits used for vertical firing.

Boucle tower.

The part of the rampart between the King's tower and the Boucle tower was built by Robert Jolivet from 1417 to 1420.

The Liberty tower has a chimney for the evacuation of gas, an innovation due to improvements in artillery.

The Boucle tower is a spur-shaped bastion built on four levels which excited Vauban's admiration. Based on a pentagonal plan, it juts out towards the enemy, and makes possible cross-fire with the next towers without any dead angle.

At last, the fort, the defensive construction of the abbey, is closed by a portcullis. It opens onto the Pit steps. It consists of corbelled towers crowned by battlemented terraces. The open space below is defended by a barbican topped with a watchpath.

In the 16th century, Gabriel du Puy, a *Gabriel tower.* King's lieutenant, built on the west side a tower which is now called Gabriel tower. It was topped with a windmill in the 17th century. He had a new barbican and the guard-room for the rich citizens built in front of the Boulevard Gate.

TIDES

With a range which can reach fifteen metres, the bay is the theater of the largest tides in Europe : the tide can go out as far as eighteen kilometres from the Mount. The tidal wave can come in as fast as ten kilometres per hour. Nowadays, the Mount is no longer surrounded by water except when it is new or full moon with a coefficient of at least 90.

THE BAY

While gazing at the bay, the eye opens on to the infinite. The light, as it moves, reveals a changing scenery with shades now silvery, now golden. The light plays on a bay which it outlines and redraws as hours go by. Sometimes sulky, it vanishes and lets the haze clothe the bay with a mysterious veil.

Haven for migratory birds, grazing ground for « pré-salé » (salted pastures) sheep, the bay generously offers its wealth of mussels, oysters, shrimps and fish.

Photo : Daniel Quérel

THE SILTING UP

The silting up of the bay, a natural phenomenon common to all the bays, has been increased here by man who has tried to reclaim lands from the sea by building dykes. The Duchess Ann's dyke was edified as early as the 11th century to isolate Dol marshes. The devastating floods of the Couesnon and the breaches that its wandering course used to open frightened the inhabitants. It was controlled and canalized by the Dutchmen and the Western polders company on about 1856. Draining projects increased at that time and brought to new agricultural land. The process of silting up will be again increased by the building of a causeway in 1879 : The Mont-Saint-Michel will no longer be encircled by the sea.

By now, every year, a million and a half cubic metres of sediment form a deposit on the bay, one which grows two centimetres higher every year.
Halophytic plants, fitted for a marine environment, hold back and fix the slimy sea-sand called « tangue », and little by little, pastures gain a hold on the sandy strands. These grassy shores (called «herbus ») move 25 or 30 hectares forward every year.

Photo : SMET - CDT 50 - André Mauxion

RECONQUEST OF THE SITE

At the dawn of the third millenium, in 2004, the project to restore the maritime feature of Mont-Saint-Michel should be realized. Its purpose is to restore the site, to give it its nobleness back and to stop the progress of the « herbus ».

The last kilometre of the causeway which leads to the ramparts will be pulled down and replaced by a bridge. As high as the causeway, it will bend towards the west and will stop a hundred metres before the Mount. The part of the ramparts which has been hidden by the causeway will then become visible. A flying-bridge will give access to the Mount entrance even when the sea encircles the Mount. Car parks will be removed and resited away in the Morvan Enclos, two kilometres away from the Mount. For those who would like it, a little train will provide a link between the car park and the Mount. A pedestrian route will allow visitors to stop and gaze at the landscape while walking towards the Mount.

To prevent the advance of « herbus », the Couesnon will recover its hydraulic power : works will be carried out at the mouth, at the Caserne Barrage, so that the tide can enter. Water will be held back then released in order to achieve the same flush as during the autumn floods.

The development coordinator is the joint syndicate for the restoration of the maritime nature of Mont-Saint-Michel. It is composed of the region of Lower-Normandy, the county of Manche and the town of Mont-Saint-Michel. The budget is about 550 million francs. The Estate is providing the major part of the financing of the project. The region of Brittany and the county of Ille-et-Vilaine also bring financial support to the joint syndicate. The project manager, appointed by the government, together with the Mont-Saint-Michel commission, will provide the technical and administrative development of the project.

Photo : Père Fr. Lancelot

« Do you have beauty, this path which leads your heart up to the sacred mountain, amongst things made of wood and stone ? »

Khalil Gibran